JUAN RAMÓN JIMÉNEZ

FIFTY SPANISH POEMS

JUAN RAMÓN JIMÉNEZ

Fifty Spanish Poems

With English translations

by

J. B. TREND

UNIVERSITY OF CALIFORNIA PRESS
BERKELEY AND LOS ANGELES
1951

This lunar beauty
Has no history
Is complete and early.

W. H. AUDEN

A trained, a choice, an exquisite appreciation of the most simple and universal relations of life . . . A rose in a moonlit garden, the shadow of trees on the turf, almond bloom, scent of pine, the wine-cup and the guitar ; these and the pathos of life and death, the long embrace, the hand stretched out in vain, the moment that glides for ever away, with its freight of music and light, into the shadow and hush of the haunted past, all that we have, all that eludes us, a bird on the wing, a perfume escaped on the gale—to all these things we are trained to respond, and the response is what we call literature.

G. LOWES DICKINSON

INDEX

JUAN RAMÓN JIMÉNEZ

POETRY in Spanish has always attracted minds which are alert and imaginative. Some readers, even, were first drawn to the language by its poetry. Yet contemporary poetry in Spanish only began to attract general attention with the Civil War of 1936-39, and the murder of Federico García Lorca. The result has been a tendency to take Lorca for the only Spanish poet of his time, though actually he was a younger member of a brilliant school and a flourishing modern tradition, represented in other fields by the well-known names of Falla, Casals and Picasso. In Spanish poetry to-day, the central figure is Juan Ramón Jiménez.

The poets, like the musicians and the painters, have been scattered by the Civil War and the persecution which followed it. Antonio Machado died of pneumonia in the Pyrenees, escaping in midwinter from Barcelona; Miguel Hernández died of consumption in prison. The rest are exiles in North or South America, and one of the best collections of contemporary Spanish poetry appeared in Chile in 1943 under the name of "Poets in exile," *Poetas en el destierro*. Among the things destroyed by the military revolt was a poetic revival, more intense than any known in Spain for three hundred years.

All the poets of that school, and all the writers who were their friends, were descended from the Spanish and Spanish-American *modernistas* of 1898; but they had grown out of the original *modernismo* and were reacting against it. For *modernismo*, in spite of its name (or because of it), had dated; and by 1928 there was little of it left beyond its effect on the technique of writing Spanish verse. This poetry could not fail to be affected by the symbolists. One of the chief symbols had been the swan—the swan of Baudelaire and Verlaine and Yeats; but Juan Ramón

Jiménez once remarked that the swan on dry land is a goose: *El cisne en tierra es ganso;* and in the end it was a Mexican poet, Enrique González Martínez, who—remembering Verlaine and what he had said about rhetoric—called on all Spanish-speaking poets to wring the swan's neck, though he did so in a sonnet of those alexandrines which owed their form to Rubén Darío, the chief poet in Spanish of the swan whose neck he was wringing.

All the tendencies of *modernismo*—the new things the poets were saying and the new forms in which they were saying them—were to be found in the poetry of Rubén Darío, who was born in the Central American republic of Nicaragua, but eventually became the most cosmopolitan poet who had ever written in Spanish. Some of the forms, and verses of much the same kind, had been used in Spanish-speaking America before, e.g. by Gutiérrez Nájera in Mexico, by José Asunción Silva in Colombia and by Julio del Casal in Cuba; while an earlier, romantic Argentine poet, Esteban Echeverría, has now and then a line which sounds more modern than anything to be heard at that time in Spain.* There were, however, in Spain towards the end of the century, that delicate, premature child of French symbolism, Gustavo Adolfo Bécquer, and another Andaluz, Salvador Rueda, each in his own way looking forward to the new poetry of the end of the century; while there was something of the same feeling in the clear Catalan poems of Jacint Verdaguer and the misty Celtic longing of Rosalía de Castro, whether she wrote in ringing Castilian Spanish or in her own wistful, Galician dialect of Portuguese.

Many of the ideas of the new poetry, if not the forms, were there in the rough-hewn verses of Unamuno. Unamuno was inclined to write poetry—and in particular sonnets—as if he were heaving half a brick at a wall, writing verse (Keats once said) "with all its lines abrupt and angular":† but in the end it was Unamuno the thinker, even more than Rubén Darío the prosodist—*modernismo ideal* rather than *modernismo formal*—who raised the stale, conventional poetry of the Spanish nineteenth century to the level it

*P. Henríquez Ureña, *La versificación irregular en la poesía española.* 2nd ed. (1933), p. 318.

†"Trató todo lo divino y lo humano, como buen vasco, a pedradas y juramentos, y lo quiso arreglar todo a su modo." (J.R.J.)

had reached in 1935, and Darío himself once declared that Unamuno was before all things a poet.

The effects, the convergence of " Unamuno within and Rubén Darío without," were at once apparent in Antonio Machado. Juan Ramón Jiménez, who knew Machado well, remembers the strong influence on him at that time of certain poems of Rubén Darío: *Retratos, Cosas del Cid, Cyrano en España;* and that northern corner of Madrid, where the first University College was afterwards built—the *Residencia de Estudiantes* with which they were both to be so closely connected—" will well remember the enthusiastic declamation of Antonio Machado . . . when we walked there together on summer evenings." The second wave came in the 1920's, when the younger poets looked back, and up, to Góngora, Garcilaso and Gil Vicente, the three sixteenth century masters whose Renascence technique and humanist thought had tightened up the tension of Spanish poetry to make it a satisfactory modern instrument; while all the time, the still small voice of Bécquer continued to be heard by really sensitive poetic natures. Antonio Machado heard it in the winding *Galerías* of his own mind; and Juan Ramón Jiménez heard it, while with his fine poetic sensibility, his keen eye, his alert ear and his strangely beautiful handwriting, he continued the new movement in Spanish poetry and eventually spread it to all the twenty countries where Spanish is spoken.

Juan Ramón Jiménez, born in 1881, was already publishing poems by 1898. For him, *modernismo* was part of the general movement for freedom from romanticism—literary, artistic, scientific, social and religious—which had begun in Spain and Spanish-speaking America about the same time. In Spain the movement of thought and feeling owed much to the teaching, encouragement and friendliness of Don Francisco Giner de los Ríos at the " Free School," the *Institución Libre de Enseñanza,* and the University college, the *Residencia de Estudiantes*; and it is surprising how many of the later poets have been connected with these institutions.

Juan Ramón Jiménez has worked at poetry consistently throughout his life, either writing new poems or polishing and refining poems already published. He has done many of the things which his

Spanish contemporaries have done, but he did them first. The famous " green " poem of García Lorca :

Verde que te quiero, verde,

had several forerunners in the older poet. There is, for instance, *Verde, verderol,* the poem of a greenfinch, written about 1907 and reprinted in the volume called *Canción* in 1936. It has proved untranslatable, though the refrain might be imitated, more or less,

A bird so green
was never seen.

But that will not do ! This is the verbal magic of a nursery rhyme, something in the manner of Walter de la Mare (and of James Joyce, too, who also was haunted by childish jingles) ; and it has defied all attempts to reproduce it in English. Such verbal magic runs through the whole work of Juan Ramón Jiménez, but he has had the tact never to depend on it too much. It is found in two of the poems included in the second edition of the Oxford Book of Spanish Verse : *Dios está azul* (God's blue to-day) and *Almoradú del monte* (*Marjoram up on the mountain*), and they, too, have resisted repeated attempts to turn them into English. We might try

Here we go round and round for rosemary,
here we go, here we go,
round for rosemary and for love.

But that does not represent the Spanish, or give the full effect of it.

¡ Vámonos al campo por romero,
vámonos, vámonos
por romero y por amor !

Few people realize that Spanish lends itself to verbal magic, to nursery rhymes—and even nonsense rhymes—like English. One of the most surprising, in this century, is the Cuban poet Mariano

Brull. He too has a " green " poem;—with the charm and inconsequence of a nursery rhyme.

> Por el verde, verde
> verdería de verde mar
> Rr con Rr . . .
>
> Rr con Rr
> en mi verde limón
> pájara verde.
>
> Por el verde, verde
> verdehalago húmedo
> extiéndome.—Extiéndote.
>
> Vengo de Mundodolido
> y en Verdehalago me estoy.

Verbal magic, certainly; but nonsense ? Not quite. It is what anyone would feel to-day, if they went to sleep in post-war Europe and woke up in Cuba.

> Vengo de Mundodolido
> y en Verdehalago me estoy.

That was written about 1916, earlier than anything of García Lorca.

Another " green " poem, however, will go into English rather better—well enough, at any rate, to give an idea of what the original is like—*La verdecilla, El pajarito verde,* The little green bird (1).

This leads back to the delicate art of *La castigada* (Francina's garden) a piece of sensuous impressionism which belongs to the time (1908) and place (France) of the impressionist piano-pieces of Debussy, like *Jardins sous la pluie.* Francina—and this poem is the sole survivor of seven early poems in the *Poemas mágicos y dolientes* of 1909—had apparently been sun-bathing in a French garden when the poet came out and caught her (2).

Debussy's piece is written round two popular French tunes; Juan Ramón Jiménez's poem is written, like many of his poems, in the popular 8-syllable verse of Spanish ballad-metre, with its " hovering stresses," its characteristically varied accentuation. But another measure was running in his head: the tropical alexandrine of Rubén Darío. It seemed new in Spanish, or not quite naturalized, and must have sounded no less strange than the English alexandrines written about 1890 by Lionel Johnson :

> The night is full of stars, full of magnificence,
> Nightingales hold the wood, and fragrance loads the dark ;

or the more Spenserian

> Flung round him trumpet-toned about his clear domains.

This was followed, in 1899, by the new music of Yeats :

> With heavy whitening wings and a heart fallen cold . . . .
> Desolate winds that cry over the wandering sea,

—music which seemed to come from

> lands that seem too dim to be burdens on the heart.

Juan Ramón Jiménez wrote much in this metre, beginning with experimental Spanish versions from the *Stances* of *Moréas*—a poet who could sometimes fly, with Lucretius,

> A l'azur étoilé de ces flambeaux errants.

—and the beautiful, languid verses of Samain's *Jardin de l'Infante*, where

> . . . chaque feuille d'or tombe, l'heure venue,
> Ainsi qu'un souvenir, lente, sur le gazon ;

where

> Le Séraphin des soirs passe le long des fleurs,

and

> . . . Le dernier rayon agonise à tes bagues.

Again, in 1907, he tells us that he was haunted by the strange and unexpected beauty of the *Nuits de Juin* of Victor Hugo,

> L'été, lorsque le jour a fui, de fleurs couverte
> La plaine verse au loin un parfum enivrant . . .

Alexandrines appear in the *Elejías* (1907-8), *La Soledad sonora* (1908)—that " solitude filled with sound " which he christened from Juan de la Cruz—and in some of the *Poemas agrestes* (1912), *Laberinto* and *Melancolía* (1910-11), and *Apartamiento* (1911-12) He used them also for the translation of some lines of Shelley. These poems are not strictly " modernistas," in the original Spanish or Spanish-American sense; they are mainly elegiac poems, with the ghost of the Latin elegiac couplet peeping from behind the rhymed Spanish alexandrines. The " spectral fixity " of these elegies achieves, however, one thing that Rubén Darío once or twice attempted for his own tropical country of Nicaragua, but rarely accomplished. The southern heat and light become real; we are oppressed and dazzled, in *Mar del Sur* (3).

In this early period Juan Ramón Jiménez was describing objects by the method of enrichment, not of economy—by crowded sensations and by words consciously poetic and chosen. The poetry of Yeats, too, passed through an analogous phase. Juan Ramón Jiménez, in this style, has a wonderful evocation of a cathedral in the south of Spain, *Catedral del pueblo* (6). In " The Bay of Delusion " he does more by suggestion than by description: the boats, by now invisible, are shown in outline by the little coloured lanterns which illuminated them for the gala-night, the tiny suns of amber, red and purple reflected in the sea.

> Barcos, no se veían. Sólo los farolillos
> colorados, morados, amarillos, pintaban
> las jarcias invisibles, con soles amarillos,
> morados, colorados, que las aguas doblaban.

By now the gala had shed the petals of all its blossoms. A great, clean all-pervading silence had fallen. And then the bitter, thirsting upheaval of the sunrise brought back to one shore and the other its hopelessness.

> Ya la fiestas habían deshojado sus flores,
> y un gran silencio limpio, contenido, se oía . . .
> que el amargo trastorno sediento de la aurora
> fijó luego, en un lado y en otro, tristemente.

The poet can convey the same sort of impression, by much the same method, for snow-scenes too: *Estampa de invierno* (4). Island, *Isla* (5) is more personal in its approach.

The elegiac mood was relieved by satire, though that too is presented in the same elegiac metre. There is delightful mockery in the music-lesson given by one of the nuns in a convent (*Clase*) :

¡Sevillanas en claustro mudéjar! Qué piano
Pleyel . . . de Barcelona! ¡Debussy! En tres semanas,
Solfeo— ¡gracia inútil de la cansada mano!—
Clave de fa, armonía y luego . . . ¡Sevillanas!
—¡Monjas en sevillana! ¡Oh cercana Sevilla! . . .

Dancing nuns in a Moorish cloister! What a piano!
Pleyel, from Barcelona. Debussy ? In three weeks' lessons,
Sight-reading ? Useless accomplishment ; tires the hands so !
Key of one flat, simple harmony, then . . . Sevillanas !
Nuns dancing Sevillanas ! Well, we're almost in Seville ! . . .

Or there is the pious old woman, called in Spain a *beata :* " The Old Woman at the Bank " (Banquera)—bank in the sense of the musical banks in Samuel Butler's *Erewhon*, which were not the banks that we know, but churches.

Se guarda los recibos en el seno. ¡Si fuera
el cielo un banco, y las estrellas pesetas fijas . . . !

She puts away the vouchers in her bosom. If only
Heaven were a bank, and all the stars were pegged pesetas !

These were entitled *alejandrinos de cobre*, alexandrines of copper alluding, perhaps, to that sinister character in the Pauline Epistles, Alexander the Coppersmith. The satires were called *poesías al revés*, poems inside out. Many who have read (and some who have written on) the poetry of Juan Ramón Jiménez have overlooked them, though they are an important part of his character. " Spain," he has said,* " is a country which, taken all in all, is deeply realist and falsely religious, Catholic rather than Christian, ecclesiastical rather than spiritual, a country of roots and feet rather than of wings ; and the true poetry of Spain, the only possible kind of written lyric poetry, was begun by the feelings of Everyman (*el sentir del pueblo*) and by the few strange mystics,

***Poesía y literatura.* Hispanic American Studies, 2. University of Miami, 1944).

whose landscape was the sullen rock and the marvellous sky. They all try to fly, naturally; and for that reason the best Spanish lyrics have been, and are, inevitably mystical, with God or without him; for the poet is a mystic, though he does not necessarily have a god."

It should be made quite clear that there is nothing in Juan Ramón Jiménez of that conventional Andalucian pose called *popularismo*, so worked to death by foreign writers on Spain, and indeed important in the poetry of Villalón and García Lorca; though there, it is transfigured and transformed into something deeper and more tragic, and much more fundamentally Spanish. Lorca appears in his poems something more than "the mean sensual man" (and considerably more than he actually was in real life); and that, too, has been taken for a Spanish characteristic, like his preoccupation with death—which is not really Spanish but religious. That again is *popularismo*. All three poets had fine, sensitive natures, sensual in the best sense; but the most sensitive is undoubtedly Juan Ramón Jiménez. In Villalón there is real poetry—not (it has been mistakenly assumed) poetry of the bull-ring, but of the vast *dehesas:* the pastures where bulls are bred; the poetry of the breeder, superbly mounted, with nothing but the long grass and the sky, and a *garrocha*, or short lance, in his hand in case of accident. Villalón was a cattle-breeder. His ambition, he declared, was to breed a bull with green eyes; and he lost a fortune over it. But he wrote interesting poetry; and after *Romances del* 800 in the earlier manner of García Lorca, he made a sensation in the late 'twenties with poetry of a completely modern cut.

Juan Ramón Jiménez, from copying or describing what he saw, or allowing its existence to be deduced from what he said, came to occupy himself not with objects but with the way light fell upon them. In this he was following the familiar road of the painters—he, too, had once thought of being a painter—who have passed from painting objects to painting light itself. The poem *Last Light* (12) combines this pictorial technique with an exquisite, dancing movement of the lines. The English version given here is a clumsy imitation; but it may show how the original was meant to go, in the way that R. C. Trevelyan's translations of Greek choruses show the movement of the original Greek. If this be rejected for mere virtuosity, or mere prettiness, the next poem (which demanded no less technical address in the original Spanish), is a true lyric, a moment of vision (13).

It is not true that " poems that are written in one language can only be enjoyed by a particular race or nationality." Such poems are not poems in any true sense ; for the genuine quality of poetry does not depend on the language in which it is written. The object of a translation from Juan Ramón Jiménez should not be to produce a second-hand poem in English on the same subject, but to convey in English the exotic impression of the original poem in Spanish. The translation, Trevelyan says, should be " disinfected " from all English associations. A poem is bound to lose much in translation ; Cervantes said that it was like looking at the wrong side of a tapestry. But sometimes—in Arthur Waley's translations from the Chinese classics, and Harold Acton's versions from Chinese contemporaries—translation can be made very well worth while, even allowing that a large proportion of the total effect of the poem will appear to be lost, to one who can understand it in its own language.

This seems particularly true of Juan Ramón Jiménez's sonnets : the *Sonetos espirituales* written in 1914-15. In an English version the rhymes must often be sacrificed ; that was the poet's own method, he tells us, in translating Samain and Moréas into Spanish ; for even if it were possible to produce a rhymed version of reasonable accuracy, the rhyming sounds would have no relation to the rhymes of the original. Spanish is believed to be an " easy " language ; but the scientific, phonetic fact remains that not *one* of the Spanish sounds is exactly the same as the corresponding sound in English. Yet the rhythm and movement of the language can be imitated, and something recognizable will be carried over in a translation. Poetry does not really depend on the colour or vowel-harmony or beauty of the original verbal sounds, but on the colour of the poetic emotions ; and in most modern poetry the nuance of the poetic emotions is more important than the nuance of the words. Rhyme and regularity, a Chinese poet told Harold Acton, may be not only disadvantageous to poetic emotion ; they may distort it. But the movement, one may add, is something permanent.

The last sonnet of the three (16) looks forward to Heidegger and Sartre. But Spaniards do not need Heidegger to make them existentialists; that outlook—or what is essential in that outlook—is theirs by nature, and without conscious strain. This particular sonnet is near to the later Antonio Machado; but here again Juan Ramón Jiménez was first. It is unnecessary to look at it through the spectacles of dogmatic theology or describe it in the jargon of modern mysticism; for it expresses something fundamentally Spanish: a feeling which all genuine Spaniards have somewhere within them—the threat of the ineluctable, felt so strongly by Unamuno.

In form, the *Sonetos espirituales* revive (that good critic and good friend, Díez-Canedo saw) the direct inspiration of the Spanish sonneteers of the sixteenth century, without the complication of the seventeenth or the bombast of the nineteenth; they have no surprise in store in the last verse, nor any rhymes which are unusual. But the poet was seeking a simpler form of expression. Alexandrines and hendecasyllables seemed too "baroque"; and among a good deal of poetry in prose, he wrote the marvellous prose-study *Platero y yo*, published in 1914. Platero (the name means, literally "silversmith") was the poet's donkey. It was still almost before the days of cars, in those parts. People in the South of Spain habitually rode on donkeys, and looked after them like Sancho Panza looking after his *rucio*, Dapple. Yet the principal character is neither Platero nor Juan Ramón; it is the whole population of a white, gleaming town in Andalucía: Moguer, the poet's birthplace; one of those small seaports from which the caravels of Columbus set out for China and discovered America.

Juan Ramón Jiménez had been reading Yeats and "A.E." and Blake, and translating Synge's *Riders to the Sea;* but the poems written in 1915 and published in *Estío* (Summer) were not influenced by the Anglo-Irish poets, or by his wife's attractive Spanish versions of Rabindranath Tagore. They show him, however, experimenting in free verse, or rather, verses of different length following one another irregularly, for it is difficult to find a line of Juan Ramón Jiménez which is not a genuine Spanish verse of some kind. He abandoned rhyme, and fell back on the traditional

Spanish assonance, which Spanish poets have been using continuously for eight hundred years.

Next came a visit to America, and a happy marriage. America in itself made little outward effect on Juan Ramón Jiménez. There was no violent reaction in his poetry, though there was, later, with García Lorca. The chief effects were made by the Atlantic crossings; and the *Diario de un poeta recién casado,* in verse and prose, is mainly a book of the sea. New York, though it did not have the effect on him it had on other Spanish poets, was nevertheless the inspiration of one of his finest poems (22). It was dedicated to Antonio Machado. The reference to Washington Square should be considered with the date: 1916; it is the Washington Square of Henry James, rather than of to-day. There is a fine poem, too, on New York harbour, dedicated to the memory of Enrique and Amparo Granados, the brilliant composer and his wife, who had left New York not long before, and were on board the *Sussex* when she was torpedoed in mid-channel. It is dated "New York, at my window in 11th Street, 27 March, 1916, before dawn and in yellow moonlight."

The time came for packing up and returning to Spain, and in "an empty room with trunks all fastened, 6th June (night) 1916," he wrote his poem of farewell (24). The voyage back began with two difficult and puzzling poems: *Convexities* (25) and *Rose of the Sea* (26); but by June 15th he was at work on an important poem *Partida* (Departure), of which he afterwards made an admirable gramophone record for the Centro de Estudios Históricos at Madrid (27). It was so far his longest and most ambitious single poem, but was followed by several collections of shorter poems: *Eternidades,* for instance, published in 1916-17, and *Piedra y cielo* (Rock and sky) 1917-18. *Inteligencia* (29) is typical. But what kind of poetry ought one to pursue? Not "pure" poetry, whatever that was. Juan Ramón Jiménez regarded the quest for pure poetry, in France, a wrong road, like that pseudo-religious pride in self-abasement, squalor and an unwashen body, which had so great an influence on the poetry of Verlaine and Rimbaud. Poetry was a state of mind, the symbolists said: *de l'âme pour l'âme, résumant tout, parfums, sons, couleurs;* poetry should not be pure, but naked (30). The bare precision of the word, faithful to the absolute precision of the thought; something, Yeats said,

> Where passion and precision have been one.

The sea continued to haunt him (39, 40, 41), and the idea of poetic inspiration (33, 42, 50). No. 32 refers to Dante and the sonnet, and the way that poetic ideas pass from one poet, one basin, to another, from the original source—a notion which looks back to Plotinus.

He had already made a collection of his poems for the Hispanic Society of America, published in a limited edition in 1917. This he revised and increased in the *Segunda Antolojía Poética* (1898-1918) published in Madrid in 1922. The title-page bears the date MCMXX; the book was put together during the year 1919, and the prologue—a letter to his friend Manuel G. Morente, who had asked for a selection of the poems for the Colección Universal—was signed in December. Printing began in 1920, but the impression was not ready until 1922. Few poets can have taken such care of the printing of their works, or so gracefully have thanked their publishers and printers for " the amiability and the exquisite patience with which they have borne for two and a half years the sentimental and intellectual demands of the author, excessive and useless though they may be." The fact remains that Juan Ramón Jiménez has raised the level of fine printing throughout the Spanish-speaking world.

The volumes called *Poesía* (*en verso*) and *Belleza*, in which he showed himself alert to the newest tendencies in the poetry of the time, were published in 1924. From then, down to 1936, the flow of limited and privately-printed editions continued; while *Poesía y prosa*, a selection for children—of all ages—appeared in 1934, and *Canción*, a collection of many new poems and revisions of earlier ones, in the summer of 1936.

Juan Ramón Jiménez has puzzled his friends and critics by his corrections—ruthless corrections, sometimes—of poems already published. This is not merely an effort to make an immature or imperfectly expressed poem into a better one. It may be that the poet had in mind a consistent idea which provided him with a touchstone for judging the value of all the poems he had written.

It would be inaccurate, or unwarranted, to call this view pantheist: his view of nature is not that of Shelley or Wordsworth, or even of Lucretius; but he is content, often enough, with a landscape without human figures. Perhaps the best comparison is with the paintings of Turner; but he might also be compared with the painters of China. He seems gradually to have become aware of a force of nature residing in all things, in a tree, a mountain or a woman; and he might say, like a Chinese philosopher, that an almond tree or a moonlit mountain can be alive—not like a man or an animal, or a tree, but alive with the life proper to it—and that the poem will be alive too if any of the cosmic force, the *tao*, is in it. The alterations made in the original texts of the poems, then, are not merely to make the lines run more smoothly, or the thought clearer; they seem to depend on the poet's view of the whole body of his poetry in an expression of nature. This may not be the true explanation, but it is safe to say that the changes have not been made capriciously.

On the outbreak of Civil War he remained in Madrid, making himself useful in what ways he could, and in particular collecting homeless children out of the streets and reading to them in his own flat. Don Francisco Giner would have done the same. But when the time came for all those to leave Madrid whose presence there was not strictly necessary, he went to America, living for a time in Havana, and then in Florida. Some poems have undoubtedly been lost, and the manuscripts of others stolen; but a reprint of the *Segunda Antolojía* appeared in Buenos Aires in 1944 and a new collection, *La estación total, con las Canciones de la nueva luz* in 1946.

In *Poesía* (*en verso*) and *Belleza*, Juan Ramón Jiménez was seeking poetry in new places, "the beauty that's undesigned and tardy—always there for the improvident"; in the no-man's land of *Dawn outside the walls*, for instance (44). *Peace* (46), however, is a strangely moving and beautiful poem; while *Rose of the Shadows* (49), and above all the first of the two poems called *Pacto* (48), represent his original and highly individual genius at one of its highest points. They had appeared in various anthologies, particularly in the fine collection of contemporary Spanish poetry edited by Gerardo Diego, *Poesía española*, 1915-31;

but were only collected by the poet himself in *La estación total* in 1946.

Juan Ramón Jiménez has also published admirable prose. Not only *Platero y yo*, which has gone into several editions in several different countries, but newer prose, prose unlike anything which had been written in Spanish before, the pieces which were collected and published in Buenos Aires in 1942: *Españoles de tres mundos*. They are portraits of Spanish people, composed over a long period of years; but among them the portraits which remain in the memory, more than all the others, are those of Don Francisco Giner and Don Manuel Cossío.

In many Spanish-speaking countries since the Civil War, and also in Portugal, the traveller finds (when people know him well enough to trust him) that the Spain now really respected is not the Spain of *hispanidad* (and all that that implies) but the Spain of Don Francisco, the Institución Libre de Enseñanza, and the Residencia de Estudiantes. This (we mentioned before) has been the home of nearly all the good modern poets: Antonio Machado, J. Moreno Villa, Alfonso Reyes, Pedro Salinas, Jorge Guillén, F. García Lorca, Emilio Prados. Unamuno, too, was often to be found at the Residencia when he was in Madrid after his return from exile in 1931, while Juan Ramón Jiménez had been one of its earliest inhabitants; he designed and planted the little gardens which lay between the college buildings—the *pabellones*—and left his influence to pervade the place . . . until its "urbanization," and the clumsy addition of extra storeys, carried out by the present regime. Juan Ramón Jiménez is probably not the only *residente* who would never again wish to see the vulgarization which has been committed on the things he loved so well and to which his presence meant so much. For nearly twenty-five years he had lived in Madrid for preference; the *andaluz* of Andalucía had become the *andaluz universal*. Though he demanded peace and quiet in his own house, he could tolerate the bleating taxi-cabs of the *Centro* of Madrid, when they drove an English acquaintance to distraction. "*El rebaño*," he remarked: "the herd"; and the English acquaintance caught a vision, not only of Don Quixote and the armies which were sheep, but of all the ages of Castille, with the migratory shepherds and vast herds of lowing cattle of the Mesta, jostling one another along a *cañada real.* Juan Ramón Jiménez is not, then, a recluse who would avoid the centre of a big city or be unable to see the poetry in it; but he would avoid, and has always avoided, everything that could be described and condemned by the word *basto.* In that, he was like Cossío; no one who ever heard them pronounce that word could ever forget it, or fail to realize what they felt. The truth is that those institutions to which Cossío and Juan Ramón Jiménez belonged bred the intellectual honesty, without which no one—in Spain or in any other country—can ever become a really good poet, and the sensitive alertness to the presence of poetry which Yeats once called the " touch from behind the curtain."

J. B. TREND.

List of editions consulted.

JARDINES LEJANOS. (Madrid, 1904)
ELEGÍAS I. ELEGÍAS PURAS. (Madrid, 1908)
ELEGÍAS II. ELEGÍAS INTERMEDIAS—1908. (Madrid, 1909)
ELEGÍAS III. ELEGÍAS LAMENTABLES—1908. (Madrid, 1910)
BALADAS DE PRIMAVERA. (Madrid, 1910)
POEMAS MÁGICOS Y DOLIENTES—1909. (Madrid, 1911)
PASTORALES—1905. (Madrid, 1911)
LA SOLEDAD SONORA—1908. (Madrid, 1911)
MELANCOLÍA—1910-11. (Madrid, 1912)
OBRAS DE JUAN RAMÓN JIMÉNEZ. SONETOS ESPIRITUALES (1914-15). (Madrid, Calleja, 1916)
DIARIO DE UN POETA RECIÉN CASADO, 1916. (Madrid, Calleja, 1916)
ESTÍO. (Madrid, Calleja, 1916)
PLATERO Y YO. (1907-1916). (Madrid, Calleja, 1917)
POESÍAS ESCOJIDAS (1899-1917). (New York, Hispanic Society of America, 1917)

EL JIRASOL Y LA ESPADA, I. JOHN M. SYNGE. JINETES HACIA EL MAR. Juan Ramón Jiménez y Zenobia Camprubi de Jiménez, editores de su propia y sola obra. (Madrid, 1920)

ANTOLOJÍA SEGUNDA POÉTICA (1898-1918). Colección Universal Calpe. (Madrid-Barcelona, 1922)

BELLEZA (en verso). (1917-1923). Juan Ramón Jiménez y Zenobia Camprubí de Jiménez, editores de su propia y sola obra. (Madrid, 1923)

POESÍA (en verso). (1917-1923). Juan Ramón Jiménez y Zenobia Camprubí de Jiménez, editores de su propia y sola obra. (Madrid, 1923)

1925. (Madrid, 1925). (Privately printed)

OBRA EN MARCHA. (Diario poético). (Madrid, 1928)

ETERNIDADES—VERSO—1916-17. (Madrid, 1931)

SUCESIÓN, 1-8. (Madrid, 1932)

POESÍA EN PROSA Y VERSO (1902-1932), escojida para los niños por Zenobia Camprubí Aymar. (Madrid, Signo, 1933)

RAMO A LOPE. (In "Treinta canciones de Lope de Vega puestas en música." Madrid, Residencia de Estudiantes, 1935).

CANCIÓN. (Madrid, Signo, 1936)

ESPAÑOLES DE TRES MUNDOS: VIEJO MUNDO, NUEVO MUNDO, OTRO MUNDO. (Buenos Aires, 1942)

SONETOS ESPIRITUALES. COLECCIÓN RAMO DE ORO. (Buenos Aires, 1942)

ESTÍO (a punta de espina). Biblioteca Contemporánea, 130. (Buenos Aires, 1944)

ETERNIDADES 1916-1917. Id., 142. (Buenos Aires, 1944)

ANTOLOJÍA POÉTICA. Id., 144. (Buenos Aires, 1944)

ANTOLOJÍA POÉTICA. (Poetas de España y América). (Buenos Aires, Losada, 1945)

BELLEZA. Id., 147. (Buenos Aires, 1945)

VOCES DE MI COPLA. (México, Nueva Floresta II, 1945)

POESÍA. Biblioteca Contemporánea, 174. (Buenos Aires, 1946)

PLATERO Y YO. Edición completa con ilustraciones de Norah Borges. (Buenos Aires, Losada, 1942; 2 ed. 1946)

LA ESTACIÓN TOTAL CON LAS CANCIONES DE LA NUEVA LUZ. (1923-1936). (Buenos Aires, Losada, 1946)

ROMANCES DE CORAL GABLES. (México, Nueva Floresta VI, 1948)

1 LA VERDECILLA

Verde es la niña. Tiene
verdes ojos, pelo verde.

Su rosilla silvestre
no es rosa ni blanca. Es verde.

¡En el verde aire viene!
(La tierra se pone verde).

Su espumilla fuljente
no es blanca ni azul. Es verde.

¡En el mar verde viene!
(El cielo se pone verde).

Mi vida le abre siempre
una puertecita verde.

Canción, 109.

2 LA CASTIGADA

. . . *Rit de la fraîcheur de l'eau.*
V. HUGO.

Con lilas llenas de agua
le golpeé las espaldas.
Y toda su carne blanca
se enjoyó de gotas claras.

¡Ay fuga mojada y cándida
sobre la arena perlada!

(La carne moría pálida
entre los rosales granas,
como manzana de plata
amanecida de escarcha).

Corría huyendo del agua,
entre los rosales granas.
Y se reía fantástica.
La risa se le mojaba . . .

Con varas de lilas y agua,
corriendo la golpeaba . . .

Canción, 75.

1 GREEN

Green was the maiden, green, green!
Green her eyes were, green her hair.

The wild rose in her green wood
was neither red nor white, but green.

Through the green air she came.
(The whole earth turned green for her).

The shining gauze of her garment
was neither blue nor white, but green.

Over the green sea she came.
(And even the sky turned green then).

My life will always leave unlatched
a small green gate to let her in.

2 FRANCINA'S GARDEN

With dripping bunches of lilac
I splashed her over the shoulder,
and over her fair white form
the jewels rolled in clear round dew-drops.

Oh, fly away, drenched and glistening,
over the beaded sand!

(The flesh would turn pale and wither
though the roses still were red,
pale as a silver apple
that dawn had dusted with hoar-frost).

She fled me, away from the water,
while the roses still were red.
How she laughed, fantastic sprite!
Her laughter itself was water.

With rods of lilac and water,
even as she ran, I beat her.

3 MAR DEL SUR

En el sopor azul e hirviente de la siesta,
el jardín arde al sol. Huele a rosas quemadas.
La mar mece, entre inmóviles guirnaldas de floresta,
una diamantería de olas soleadas.

Cúpulas amarillas encienden a lo lejos,
en la ciudad atlántica, veladas fantasías ;
saltan, ríen, titilan momentáneos reflejos
de azulejos, de bronces y de cristalerías.

El agua abre sus frescos abanicos de plata
hasta el reposo verde de las calladas hojas,
y en el silencio solitario, una fragata,
blanca y henchida, surje, entre las rocas rojas . . .

Antolojía, 111.

3 SOUTHERN SEA

In the deep blue and fevered lethargy of the siesta
the garden flames in the sun. A smell of burnt roses.
The tide heaves between the unmoving leafy garlands :
a million million diamonds gleaming from sunny waves.

Amber cupolas and towers take fire in the far distance
in an oceanic city of veiled phantasy :
leaping, laughing and twinkling ; momentary reflections
of gleaming tiles, of bronzes, of rows of crystal panes.

The water opens cooling fans of beaten silver,
deep down, as the green slumber of hushed leaves ;
and through the solitary silence moves a frigate :
white, with swelling sails, among the rocks of flame.

4 ESTAMPA DE INVIERNO

(Nieve.)

¿Dónde se han escondido los colores
en este día negro y blanco?
La fronda, negra; el agua, gris; el cielo
y la tierra, de un blanquinegro pálido;
y la ciudad doliente
una vieja aguafuerte de romántico.

El que camina, negro;
negro el medroso pájaro
que atraviesa el jardín como una flecha...
Hasta el silencio es duro y despintado.

La tarde cae. El cielo
no tiene ni un dulzor. En el ocaso,
un vago amarillor casi esplendente,
que casi no lo es. Lejos, el campo
de hierro seco.
Y entra la noche, como
un entierro; enlutado
y frío todo, sin estrellas, blanca
y negra, como el día negro y blanco.

Antolojía, 115.

4 WINTER SCENE : SNOW

Where, oh where have they hidden all the colours
on this wan day of white and black?
The foliage, black ; the water, grey ; the earth
and sky a deathly white and black pallor ;
and the dejected city
only an old romantic etching.

Men on the road are black ;
black, the frightened bird
that darts across the garden like an arrow.
Even the silence is hard and colourless.

The evening falls. The sky
has nothing of kindliness. And now at sunset
a livid yellow gleam, hardly resplendent,
or hardly a gleam at all. Out in the country,
all rust-red iron.
                        Night comes on like a funeral.
Everything is draped in mourning,
and all is cold ; no stars at all, but white
and black, just as the day is : white and black.

5 ISLA

Una soledad tan pura
como el caer de la nieve ;
un blancor divino, unánime,
un silencio permanente . . .

¡Que todos estén muy lejos!
¡Que yo mismo no me acuerde
de mí! . . . Sólo el ideal
con su avenida y su fuente.

—La fuente no saltará :
será un éstasis perene,
cual de un diamante atraído
por el sinfín del poniente ;
poniente que no ha de abrir
rojos ni ardientes verjeles,
que será una fantasía
toda en un blanco indeleble.—

¡Que nadie me venga a hablar!
¡Que yo mismo no recuerde!
. . . Una paz tan suavísima
como el caer de la nieve.

Antolojía, 134.

ISLAND

Oh, for a solitude as pure
as a fall of snow!
A whiteness all divine, unanimous :
a silence that is permanent.

I wish they were far away!
Oh, that I might not remember
even myself! The ideal alone :
a fountain and an avenue.

The fountain will not be playing ;
but in timeless ecstasy,
like a diamond reflecting
a vast, unending sunset ;
a sunset that will never open
on flaming, tropical gardens,
but will be a fantasy
all in indelible white—

Let everyone leave me alone.
I myself shall not remember.
. . . A peace, gentler, and more delicate
than a fall of snow.

6 CATEDRAL DE PUEBLO

¡Catedral pobre, al sur, en el trigo de estío,
cuando el sol puro es miel de los rosetones,
que abren a las abejas de ensueño del ocaso
su piedra maternal, en panal de colores!

¡Olvido soñoliento y puro, que idealizan
agujas encendidas, nimbos auriluzones,
donde campanas lentas, hablan, eternizadas
por su ceguera clara, de todos los entonces!

—El campo quieto, el río ondulante, el verjel
pleno, se ven más bellos desde la ardiente torre,
en la que el viento alegre cruza, entre las esquilas,
cruces de fresca luz . . .

Y visiones salobres,
rutas de gloria nueva, llegan a la penumbra
fragante y silenciosa de los quietos rincones,
en donde desteñidas arquitecturas de oro,
ruinas viejas de cielos caídos, se recojen.—

Antolojía, 160.

6 CATHEDRAL IN A COUNTRY TOWN

Cathedral far in the south in the summer wheat fields,
where the hard sunshine is honey to rose-windows,
open to all the bees of magical, dreaming sunsets,
a honeycomb of colour in soft maternal stone-work.

Forgetfulness, drowsy and innocent, made immortal
by flaming pinnacles, by gold-reflecting cloud-banks,
where every bell is slow-tongued, in tune with eternity,
in deliberate blindness to all its contemporaries.

This quiet country, winding river and well-stocked garden,
never so good, not seen from the top of the burning tower ;
and there too the cheerful breezes, meeting among the bell-strokes,
are clashes of new light . . .

And salty, sea-borne visions,
roads to a new glory, leading away to twilight
of fragrance and silence, down in the quiet corners
where discoloured, golden pieces of architecture,
ancient ruins of fallen skies, are hidden away.

7 COMO EN UN RÍO QUIETO

Como en un río quieto, en el papel la frente
refleja, quieta, las palabras
que vibran en sus cielos, cual las notas de estrellas
de un laberinto de campanas.

Notas que van formando, luz a luz, son a son,
rosa a rosa, lágrima a lágrima,
no sé qué arquitectura encendida y cantante,
ablandada de luna de alma.

Fin sin fin de una rota armonía sin nombre,
jamás, en la idea, apagada ;
hojas secas, cristales de color, flores únicas,
que, entre la sombra, se entrelazan.

Un ¿ qué ? del más allá, que llega hasta la vida
por veredas trasfiguradas,
cual una aurora errante, que en los cielos del sueño
dejase atrás polen de plata.

Antolojía, 171.

7 WAS IT A SMOOTH STREAM

Was it a smooth stream, a sheet of paper, my forehead
reflected, smoothed out all the words,
vibrating through their heavens like the voices of stars
lost in a labyrinth of bell-notes?

Notes that were slowly forming, light on light, sound on sound,
rose upon rose, tear upon tear;
some strange new architect's dream, blazing with light and singing,
mellowed by moonlight in my soul.

Endless end of a broken and nameless harmony,
never in thought to be extinguished;
those dry leaves, the flash of a crystal, one lone blossom,
deep in the shadow intermingled.

Some unknown thing from afar, that reaches down to our life here,
by winding ways of transfiguration,
like an erratic daystar coming to skies of dream-worlds,
scattering behind pollen of silver.

8 PASIÓN DE TORMENTA

¡Luz corrediza de ocasos que se barajan,
por las mojadas calles, en las tardes de lluvia!
Todo cambia. De pronto, se oscurece lo claro,
o se aclara lo oscuro.

Una lívida música
de plata en desentono, sustituye a la espléndida
armonía de oro de las celestes tubas,
—los órganos quiméricos de melodiosas ascuas,
de los ponientes puros, que no se acaban nunca.—

Miseria y cercanía. La revolución negra
del cielo echa a las playas nuestras, monstruosas pulpas.
Trastornos de alma y carne bajo el desorden alto,
nos llevan, beodos torpes, en rachas de locura.

Antolojía, 240.

9 ¡Quién sabe del revés de cada hora!
¡Cuántas veces la aurora
estaba tras un monte!
¡Cuántas el rejio hervor de un horizonte
tenía en sus entrañas de oro el trueno!
Aquella rosa era veneno.
Aquella espada dió la vida.
Yo pensé una florida
pradera en el remate de un camino,
y me encontré un pantano.
Yo soñaba en la gloria de lo humano,
y me hallé en lo divino.

Antolojía, 258.

8 STORM

The night is a running curtain of sunsets, shuffled together,
down in the dripping street on a rainy afternoon.
But then all changes. The clear sky is suddenly darkened,
or else the dark becomes clear.

There is a livid music
of silver that's out of tune, instead of the splendid sound,
the golden harmony of the celestial tubas ;
great chimerical organs, bright with melodious embers
of clear-skied sunsets which never have an end.

Misery and proximity. The black revolution
in heaven throws monstrous heaps of flesh on to our beaches.
Upheavals of flesh and spirit, disorders at high altitudes,
lead us in drunken terror to gusts of real madness.

9 Who knows what's at the back of every minute!
How many times the sunrise
has happened behind a mountain!
How often the royal thrill of a new horizon
held in its golden womb a clap of thunder!
That rose was deadly poison.
That cruel sword gave life.
I dreamed of a flowery meadow
it lay at the far end of a long road—
I found myself in a marsh.
Then I dreamed of the glory of all things human,
and found myself in the divine.

10 LEVEDAD

El visillo,
en la quietud augusta y el silencio
de la tranquila madrugada,
se mueve, dulce, al aire vago . . .

—¡Instante hermoso,
que hermanas a los vivos con los muertos,
que los confundes (no se sabe
quién está muerto, ni quién vivo)
en una misma intensidad de aliento!
. . . Todo el mundo está muerto, o todo
vivo.—

Y el aire vago de la madrugada
mueve el visillo blanco
de mi ventana abierta . . .

—Parece
este moverse del visillo
la vida universal, todo el aliento
de la tierra, la fuerza
que resta, sola,
del ímpetu del astro, su ruído
por su órbita celeste.—

Y se mueve
el visillo,
al aire vago de la madrugada,
blanco . . .

—¡Plenitud de lo mínimo,
que llena el mundo, y fija
el pensamiento inmenso,
en su vaguedad—hoja
que cae, gota
que brilla,
olor que pasa . . .!

10 LIGHTNESS

My window-curtain,
in the majestic stillness and the silence
of the unruffled early morning,
moving softly to light breezes.

Oh, lovely moment
that makes the living brother to the dead,
one like another (there's no telling
which is the dead and which the living)
in the one great intensity of breathing!
. . . All the world must be dead now, or else all
living still.

And those light breezes of the early morning
move the white, waving curtain
of my wide-open window . . .

I think
this gentle movement of my curtain
is the life of the universe, all the breath
of the earth, all the strength
remaining with us
of earth's primeval impetus, the light sound
of its whirling, heavenly orbit.

And the curtain's
moving now,
in the light breezes of the early morning,
all white . . .

Oh, how full is the least thing
that fills the world, and fixes
the boundless contemplation
of such uncertainty : the leaf
that falls, the drop
that sparkles,
the scent that passes . . .!

Y el visillo,
azul ya su blancura
—que ha pasado la noche,
mirando yo su vaguedad movida—,
se mueve, dulce, aún, al aire vago.

Antolojía, 280.

11 VOZ INMENSA

A Oscar Esplá

Sólo abren la paz una campana, un pájaro . . .
Parece que los dos hablan con el ocaso.

Es de oro el silencio. La tarde es de cristales.
Mece los frescos árboles una pureza errante.
Y, más allá de todo, se sueña un río limpio
que, separando perlas, huye hacia su infinito.

¡Soledad! ¡Soledad! Todo es claro y callado.
Sólo abren la paz una campana, un pájaro . . .

El amor vive lejos. Sereno, indiferente,
el corazón es libre. Ni está triste, ni alegre.
Lo distraen colores, brisas, cantos, perfumes . . .
Nada como en un lago de sentimiento inmune.

Sólo abren la paz una campana, un pájaro . . .
Parece que lo eterno se coje con la mano

Canción, 207.

12 LUZ ÚLTIMA

Luz en la selva en sombra, ¿te has perdido?
¡Que el sol se fué, luz en la selva en sombra!
Luz, mira, ¡te has quedado
jugando con las verdes hojas!
Di, ¿qué harás ya si el sol tuyo se fué?

. . . Luz, vén a esta hoja
blanca, y mi sentimiento
oscuro, eternamente, niña rosa, dora.

Antolojía, 290.

And the curtain
that's blue now and not white
—for it has been all night now
with me, to watch its swaying uncertainty—
is moving softly, still, in the light breeze.

11 THE GREAT VOICE

Nothing troubling our peace ; only a bell and a bird singing . . .
It may be both of them are speaking with the sunset.

The silence is pure gold. The nightfall clear crystal.
A pure roving breath is swaying the cool trees.
And, far away from all else, a limpid brook is running,
dividing pearl from pearl in its flight to eternity.

Solitude! Solitude! Everything clear and hushed now
Nothing troubling our peace ; only a bell and a bird singing . . .

But love lives far off, serene and indifferent ;
the fond heart is free yet, and knows no joy or sorrow.
Colours giving it pleasure : a breeze, a touch, a sweet scent.
It swims on a calm lake immune from sentiment.

Nothing troubling our peace ; only a bell and a bird singing . . .
To hold eternity in the palm of my hand!

12 LAST LIGHT

Light, with the wood in shadow, are you lost then ?
The sun is down, light, with the wood in shadow!
Look, light, you are left alone
to play, there, with the leaves so green.
What will you do, now that your sun's left you alone ?

. . . Come to this leaf of paper,
this white leaf and my dark sorrow.
Oh, rosy-fingered one, make gold for me forever!

13 LA ESPADA

¡Qué confiada duermes
ante mi vela, ausente
de mi alma en tu débil
hermosura, y presente
a mi cuerpo sin redes,
que el instinto revuelve!

(Te entregas cual la muerte.)

Tierna azucena eres,
a tu campo celeste
trasplantada y alegre,
por el sueño solemne,
que te hace aquí, imponente,
tendida espada fuerte.

Canción, 251.

14 NADA

A tu abandono opongo la elevada
torre de mi divino pensamiento.
Subido a ella, el corazón sangriento
verá la mar, por él empurpurada.

Fabricaré en mi sombra la alborada,
mi lira guardaré del vano viento,
buscaré en mis entrañas mi sustento . . .
mas ¡ay! ¿y si esta paz no fuera nada?

¡Nada, sí, nada, nada! . . . —O que cayera
mi corazón al agua, y de este modo
fuese el mundo un castillo hueco y frío . . .—

Que tú eres tú, la humana primavera,
la tierra, el aire, el agua, el fuego, ¡todo!,
. . . ¡y soy yo sólo el pensamiento mío!

Antolojía, 326.

13 THE SWORD OF THE SPIRIT

How trustfully you lie there
under my eyes, but eluding
the spirit's hold : your fragile
fairy loveliness in contact
with my body, all unfettered,
that every instinct would stir!

(You yield yourself like death).

Delicate white lily,
transplanted happily—
to flowery fields of heaven!
The solemnity of slumber
makes you (your power a portent),
a keen-edged sword at my side.

14 NOTHING

To your abandonment I have opposed
my godlike tower of intelligence.
I climb up there ; my blood-stained heart has caused
the sea to be empurpled with its sense.

I'll manufacture dawn from my own shadow,
protect my lyre from vain and wanton winds,
search in my self for my own sustenance ; . . .
but, ah, if that sweet peace should bring me nothing!

Nothing, yes, nothing, nothing! Oh that the waters
might now receive my soul ; and in this manner
the world be one great prison, chill and naught!

For you are you ; you are the human spring,
of earth, air, water, fire—of everything ;
while I myself am nothing but my thought.

15 A UNA JOVEN DIANA

A Alberto Jiménez

El bosque, si tu planta lo emblanquece,
sólo es ya fondo de tu paz humana,
vasto motivo de tu fuga sana,
cuyo frescor tu huir franco ennoblece.

La luz del sol del día inmenso, crece
dando contra tus hombros. La mañana
es tu estela. Por ti la fuente mana
más, y el viento por ti más se embellece.

Evoco, al verte entre el verdor primero,
una altiva y pagana cacería . . .
A un tiempo eres cierva y cazadora.

¡Huyes, pero es de ti; persigues, pero
te persigues a ti, Diana bravía,
sin más pasión ni rumbo que la aurora!

Abril, 1914.

Antolojía, 332.

16 A MI ALMA

Siempre tienes la rama preparada
para la rosa justa; andas alerta
siempre, el oído cálido en la puerta
de tu cuerpo, a la flecha inesperada.

Una onda no pasa de la nada,
que no se lleve de tu sombra abierta
la luz mejor. De noche, estás despierta
en tu estrella, a la vida desvelada.

Signo indeleble pones en las cosas.
Luego, tornada gloria de las cumbres,
revivirás en todo lo que sellas.

Tu rosa será norma de las rosas;
tu oír, de la armonía; de las lumbres
tu pensar; tu velar, de las estrellas.

Antolojía, 335.

15 DIANA

The green wood, where the sole of your foot touched it,
yielded a white path for your radiant dream ;
running, you made a fugue, yourself the theme ;
never so rich a flight till you enriched it.

The light of that prodigious day turned brighter,
the time it shone of your shoulder. The whole morning
came in your wake. For you, the streams were running
faster ; the breeze with you came fresher, lighter.

I thought when I saw you in the wood so green,
pagan and proud, a-hunting you would ride ;
yet you were both the hunted and hunter too.

Fleeing, but from yourself : pursuing . . . but then
you were hunting yourself, Diana wild,
with no more point or passion than the dew.

16 THE POET TO HIS SOUL

Day after day you keep the branch protected
in case the rose may come ; you go alert
day after day, your ear warm at the gate
of your body, for the arrow unexpected.

No wave of thought can flow from non-existence
and not derive, from your receptive shade,
the larger gleam. All night, you are awake
in your particular star, to life's persistence.

On things you leave indelible impresses ;
then, turned to an afterglow upon the height,
revive in things whereon your seal is set.

Your rose shall be the pattern of all roses ;
your ear, of harmony ; of every light
your thought ; of every waking star, your state.

17 LA HORA FALSA

Me adelanté el corazón,
como si fuera un reló,
hacia la hora tranquila.

Pero no sonó la dicha
(la dicha estaba en su puesto
y aquel ardid era necio),
¡ni fué el punto nunca, nunca!

(Ya la realidad, confusa,
vivía en la hora pasada
de aquella desesperanza.)

¡Con qué dolor volví atrás
tu hora, corazón sin paz!

Canción, 208.

18 ¿NADA MÁS?

Sólo mi frente y el cielo.
Los únicos universos.
Mi frente, sólo, y el cielo.

(Entre ellos, la brisa pura,
caricia fiel, mano única
para tantas plenitudes.
La brisa, que baja y sube).

Arriba, todo el ser vivo,
todo el sueño en mi sentido,
rozando a aquel con las alas
que a su armonía él le baja.

Nada más.
(¿Acaso eres
tú la brisa que va y viene
del cielo, amor, a mi frente?)

Canción, 215.

17 SUMMER TIME

Once I put-on the time of my heart,
just as it were a watch,
set to a calmer moment.

Happiness never came near me;
my happiness stayed as it was,
unaffected by the trick;
never, never was on time!

And reality, confused,
lived by the hour that was past:
the hour of my deep despair.

And so, wearily, I put back
your hands again, o restless heart.

18 NOTHING MORE?

Only my face and the sky;
there's no other universe!
My face, alone, and the sky!

—Between them, the wind blows pure:
a fond caress, the only hand
that brings plenitude of joy:
the wind ever rising and falling—

Above me, all that has life;
all the dream I feel within me,
peopling my sense with wings
of the dream-sent harmony.

Nothing more.
Are you, perchance,
are you the wind that comes and goes,
the wind of heaven, love, on my face?

19 QUÉ CERCA YA DEL ALMA

¡Qué cerca ya del alma
la que está tan inmensamente lejos
de las manos aún!
Como una luz de estrella,
como una voz sin nombre
traída por el sueño, como el paso
de algún corcel remoto
que oímos, anhelantes,
el oído en la tierra;
como el mar en teléfono . . .

Y se hace la vida
por dentro, con la luz inestinguible
de un día deleitoso
que brilla en otra parte.

¡Oh, qué dulce, qué dulce,
verdad sin realidad aún, qué dulce!

Madrid, 17 de enero de 1916.
Diario de un poeta recién casado, 1.

19 HOW NEAR MY SOUL ALREADY

How near my soul already
something that seems immensely far away
and still out of reach!
Like the light of a star ;
like the unnamed voice
brought by a dream ; like the passing-by
of a rider in the distance
when heard by breathless listener
with ear bent to the ground ;
like the sea on the telephone . . .

Life's made like that
inside us, with the unextinguished light
of a day of pure enjoyment
that still shines elsewhere.

Oh, how sweet it was, how sweet ;
truth, but not yet real, how sweet it was!

20 NOCTURNO

¡Oh mar sin olas conocidas,
sin " estaciones " de parada,
agua y luna, no más, noches y noches!

. . . Me acuerdo de la tierra,
que, ajena, era de uno,
al pasarla en la noche de los trenes,
por los lugares mismos y a las horas
de otros años . . .
—¡Madre lejana,
tierra dormida,
de brazos firmes y constantes,
de igual regazo quieto
—tumba de vida eterna
con el mismo ornamento renovado— ;
tierra madre, que siempre
aguardas en tu sola
verdad el mirar triste
de los errantes ojos!—

. . . Me acuerdo de la tierra
—los olivares a la madrugada—,
firme frente a la luna
blanca, rosada o amarilla,
esperando retornos y retornos
de los que, sin ser suyos ni sus dueños,
la amaron y la amaron . . .

(3 de febrero.)

Diario de un poeta recién casado, 35.

20 NOCTURNE

The sea provides no well-known waves,
no stations, halts or stopping-places ;
water and moon, no more, night after night.

My thought flies to my country ;
though others owned it, it was mine :
mine when I passed in the dark night of the through train,
all of the actual places, at the old times
of other years . . .

A mother, far off, now,
a country fast to sleep,
with arms so constant and so firm ;
the peace of a nurse's lap,
—a life that's always the same,
with the same old ornaments polished up—
a mother-country, that all day
lies waiting in her longing
and love, for the dear welcome
sight of the wanderer's eyes !—

My thought flies to my country :
the olive-groves I saw before the dawn came,
clear-cut under the moonlight,
whitish or yellow or rose-red,
always awaiting the long returning traveller ;
for those, though neither born nor bred among them,
yet loved and love them still.

21 CIELO

Te tenía olvidado,
cielo, y no eras
más que un vago existir de luz,
visto—sin nombre—
por mis cansados ojos indolentes.
Y aparecías, entre las palabras
perezosas y desesperanzadas del viajero,
como en breves lagunas repetidas
de un paisaje de agua visto en sueños . . .

Hoy te he mirado lentamente,
y te has ido elevando hasta tu nombre.

(7 de febrero.)
Diario de un poeta recién casado, 43.

21

SKY

I had almost forgot you,
sky, and you were nothing
more than a vague existence formed from light ;
seen—without thinking—
by wearied eyes and shameful indolence.
And you appeared among the words there spoken
in the idle and unenthusiastic talk of a traveller
and in the oft-repeated vision of lakes
in a watery landscape seen between dream and waking.

Now I regard you with due notice,
and you have proved yourself to be worthy of your name.

22 NOCTURNO

A Antonio Machado.

. . . Es la celeste jeometría
de un astrónomo viejo
sobre la ciudad alta—torres
negras, finas, pequeñas, fin de aquello . . .—

Como si, de un mirador último,
lo estuviera mirando
el astrólogo.

Signos
exactos—fuegos y colores—,
con su secreto bajo y desprendido
en diáfana atmósfera
de azul y honda trasparencia.

¡Qué brillos, qué amenazas,
qué fijezas, qué augurios,
en la inminencia cierta
de la estraña verdad! ¡Anatomía
del cielo, con la ciencia
de la función en sí y para nosotros!

—Un grito agudo, solo, inmenso,
como una estrella errante.—

. . . ¡Cuán lejanos
ya de aquellos nosotros,
de aquella primavera de esta tarde
—en Washington Square, tranquila y dulce—,
de aquellos sueños y de aquel amor!

Diario de un poeta recién casado, 131.

22 NOCTURNE

This is celestial geometry:
an old astrologer's planning
for a great and tall city—towers
black-lined, fine-drawn, tapering, all his own—

As if, from an ultimate balcony,
all lay under the keen eye
of the astrologer.

Aspect,
ascendent, mansion and conjunction,
with every secret open and released
in the diaphanous atmosphere
of this profound deep blue transparency.

What sudden blaze, what menace,
what positions, what nativities,
in the inevitable certainty
of the exceptional truth! Anatomy
of starry heaven, the science
of their function, for us and for themselves.

A piercing cry, immense and lonely;
lone as a wandering star.—

. . . How far off, now,
from those who once were us,
in our long distant springtime, on that evening
—in Washington Square, so calm and tranquil—
who dreamed such dreams and loved with such great love.

23

HUMO Y ORO

†

Enrique y Amparo Granados.

¡Tanto mar con luna amarilla
entre los dos, España!—y tanto mar, mañana,
con sol del alba . . .—
. . . Parten,
entre la madrugada, barcos vagos,
cuyas sirenas tristes, cual desnudas,
oigo, despierto, despedirse
—la luna solitaria
se muere, rota ¡oh Poe! sobre Broadway—,
oigo despierto, con la frente
en los cristales yertos ; oigo
despedirse una vez y otra, entre el sueño
—a la aurora no queda más que un hueco
de fría luz en donde hoy estaba
la negra mole ardiente—,
entre el sueño de tantos como duermen
en su definitiva vida viva
y al lado
de su definitiva vida muerta . . .

¡Qué lejos, oh qué lejos
de ti y de mí y de todo, en esto
—los olivares de la madrugada—,
al oír la palabra alerta— ¡muerte!—
dentro de la armonía de mi alma
—mar inmenso de duelo o de alegría—,
a la luz amarilla
de esta luna poniente y sola, España!

(New York, en mi ventana a la calle 11, 27 de marzo, madrugada, con luna amarilla.)

Diario de un poeta recién casado, 81.

23 SMOKE AND GOLD

To Enrique and Amparo Granados

So much sea in the yellowing moonlight
lying between us, Spain! And so much sea to-morrow
in early morning sunshine . . .
. . . Sailing
in the wan light of daybreak, dim-seen ships
sounding their mournful sirens, naked visions ;
sleepless, I hear them take farewell.
—In solitary splendour
the moon, oh, shade of Poe! dies over Broadway—
Sleepless, I hear them, my forehead pressing
against the rigid panes ; I hear them
take farewell, once and again, amid their dreams . . .
—and now the daybreak is nothing but an empty space
in the frigid light only yesterday
the jet-black mole was glowing—
dreams in the dream of all of those now sleeping
in that part of their life that is still living
side by side
with that part of their life already dead.

How far off, oh! how far off
from you and from me they are, and from all things
—oh! olive-groves that once I saw at daybreak!
When I hear the alert given—Death!—
breaking into the harmony of my spirit
—immeasurable sea of joy and sorrow—
in the yellowing moonlight
of that pale orb that is setting lonely in Spain too!

(*New York, at my window in* 11*th Street*, 27 *March*, 1916, *before dawn and in yellow moonlight.*)

24 REMORDIMIENTO

Le taparía el tiempo
con rosas, porque no
recordara.

Una rosa distinta,
de una imprevista majia,
sobre cada hora solitaria de oro
o sombra,
hueco propicio a las memorias trájicas.

Que como entre divinas
y alegres
enredaderas rosas, granas, blancas,
que no dejaran sitio a lo pasado,
se la enredara,
con el cuerpo,
el alma.

(New York—cuarto vacío, entre baúles cerrados—, 6 de junio, noche.)

Diario de un poeta recién casado, 155.

25 CONVEXIDADES

Vuelve el cielo su espalda,
vuelve su espalda el mar, y entre ambas desnudeces,
resbala el día por mi espalda.

Lo que en el día queda,
es lo que dicen todos todo.
Nuestros tres pechos ¡Dios! están abiertos,
contra el todo de todos,
a lo que ignoran todos,
¡hacia todo!

14 de junio.

Diario de un poeta recién casado, 170.

24 REMORSE

Soon time will cover it
with roses, that there may be
no remembrance.

The roses will be different
with an unpredicted magic,
covering every lonely hour with gold
or shadow—
moment propitious for tragic memories.

And there among the fairest
and gayest
of climbing, rambling roses, white and crimson,
that leave the past no opportunity,
the body will once more
be twined about
the spirit.

(New York, empty room with trunks all fastened, 6 June, night, 1916.)

25 CONVEXITIES

The sky had its back towards me ;
the sea also turned its back, and between their naked shoulders,
the day rebounded from my shoulders too.

All that the day had left
was that which all had said before.
Are not our three bosoms open wide,
facing the all of all men,
the all which all refuse to know
of everything!

26 ROSA DEL MAR

La luna blanca quita al mar
el mar, y le da el mar. Con su belleza,
en un tranquilo y puro vencimiento,
hace que la verdad ya no lo sea,
y que sea verdad eterna y sola
lo que no lo era.
Sí.
¡Sencillez divina,
que derrotas lo cierto y pones alma
nueva a lo verdadero!
¡Rosa no presentida, que quitara
a la rosa la rosa, que le diera
a la rosa la rosa!

(15 de junio.)
Diario de un poeta recién casado, 174.

26 ROSE OF THE SEA

The moon has taken the sea from the sea
and given it back to the sea. By her rare beauty,
and by her tranquil and virginal surrender,
making truth appear to be truth no longer,
feigning a truth eternal and universal
from one that is not so.
Yes.
Divine simplicity:
to defeat the known and fill with a new spirit
the old and tried truth.
A rose that was unforeseen, and takes away
the rose from the rose itself, but then gives back
to the rose a rose.

27

PARTIDA
(*Pureza del Mar*)

Hasta estas puras noches tuyas, mar, no tuvo
el alma mía—sola más que nunca—
aquel afán, un día presentido,
del partir sin razón.
Esta portada
de camino que enciende en ti la luna,
con toda la belleza de sus siglos
de castidad, blancura, paz y gracia,
la contajia del ansia de su ausente
movimiento.
Hervidero
de almas de azucenas, que una música
celeste fuera haciendo de cristales líquidos
en varas de hialinas cimas de olas,
con una fiel correspondencia de colores
a un aromar agudo de delicias
que estasiaran la vida hasta la muerte.

. . . ¡Majia, deleite, más, entre la sombra
donde arden los brillantes ojos sostenidos,
que la visión de aquel cantado amor,
leve, sencillo y verdadero,
que no creímos conseguir ; tan cierto
que parecía el sueño más distante!—

¡Sí, sí ; así era, así empezaba
aquello ; de este modo lo veía
mi corazón de niño, cuando, abiertos
como rosas, mis ojos,
se alzaban negros desde aquellas torres
cándidas por el iris, de mi sueño,
a la alta claridad de un paraíso!

27 DEPARTURE

Before those pure unblemished nights at sea, my spirit,
more lonely now than ever, had not known
that eagerness upon the day appointed
to sail out none knew whither.

This is the gate
to the pathway lighted on the sea by moonbeams
with all their centuries of loveliness,
of chastity, of whiteness, peace and grace;
sick with longing for the absent movement
of waves now stilled.

A seething spring
and the ghosts of white lilies; a soft melody,
a heavenly sound made music in the crystal drops of spray
of wavelets toppling their translucent crests
with every colour that the rainbow matched,
with a tantalizing savour of deliciousness;
life was ecstasy then, till all was over.

Magic and pleasure; and more, there in the shadow
where certain strange bright eyes were ever burning;
more than the vision of that long-chanted love,
simple and sure and true as steel,
that love we hardly hope to find—so truly
it seemed to us a dream of far-off ages.

Yet thus it was, and thus began
our love, and in that manner I beheld it
with childish heart, when, with my eyes wide open
(round as roses, my eyes were)
they raised their glance all black from those white towers,
white in the iris of my dreamland,
to the lofty clarity of a paradise.

¡Así era aquel pétalo de cielo,
en el que el alma se encontraba,
igual que en otra ella, única y libre!
¡Esto era, esto es, de aquí se iba,
por lisas galerías de infalibles
arquitecturas de agua, tierra, fuego y aire,
como esta noche eterna, no sé a dónde,
a la segura luz de unas estrellas!
¡Así empezaba aquel comienzo sin fin, gana
matinal de mi alma
de salir, por su puerta, hacia su ignoto centro! . . .

¡Oh blancura primera, sólo y siempre
primera!
¡Marmórea realidad de la inconciente lumbre blanca!
¡Locura de blancura irrepetible!
. . . ¡Blancura de esta noche, mar, de luna!

Diario de un poeta recién casado, 175.

Even so, that petal fallen from the sky,
where, wrapped within my soul, it lay—
(like any other, it was ; separate and free).
So it was, and so it is now ; and thence it passed
through smooth-cut galleries of infallible
architecture, of water, earth, fire and air,
like this unending night, I know not whither,
led by the unfailing light of a few stars.
Even so there came the beginning without end—the morning
of the desire of the spirit,
to fly out by the door, away to her unknown home.

Oh, first white vision I saw, alone and always
as first I saw it!
Oh, marble-white reality of uncomprehending light of day!
Oh, the rightness of that whiteness ineffable!
. . . The whiteness of this night, the sea, the moon!

28 NOCTURNO

El barco, lento y raudo a un tiempo, vence al agua,
mas no al cielo.
Lo azul se queda atrás, abierto en plata viva,
y está otra vez delante.
Fijo, el mástil se mece y torna siempre
—horario en igual número
de la esfera—
a la estrellas mismas,
hora tras hora negra y verde.
El cuerpo va, soñando,
a la tierra que es de él, de la otra tierra
que no es de él. El alma queda y sigue,
siempre, por su dominio eterno.

(18 de junio.)

Diario de un poeta recién casado, 187.

29 ¡Intelijencia, dame
el nombre exacto de las cosas!
. . . Que mi palabra sea
la cosa misma,
creada por mi alma nuevamente.
Que por mí vayan todos
los que no las conocen, a las cosas ;
que por mí vayan todos
los que ya las olvidan, a las cosas ;
que por mí vayan todos
los mismos que las aman, a las cosas . . .
¡Intelijencia, dame
el nombre exacto, y tuyo
y suyo, y mío, de las cosas!

Antolojía, 409

28 NOCTURNE

The ship, both slow and fast at once, outruns the water
but not the sky.
The blue remains behind, opening to burnished silver,
with blue in front once more.
The mast swings to and fro, returning always
—like the big hand to the same hour
on the clock-face—
to the same stars as before ;
hour after hour in sable and green.
The body's left to dreaming
of the world that is his, of the other world too
that is not his. The soul remains and follows,
ever in search of her long dominion.

29

Intelligence, oh give me
the proper name for everything.
. . . So that my word be truly
the thing in itself,
created expressly for me by my soul.
That they follow my footsteps
all who have never known the nature of things ;
that they follow my footsteps
all who have forgotten the nature of things ;
that they follow, too, my footsteps
even they who have loved all things for themselves.
Intelligence, oh give me
the proper name. and *your* name,
and theirs and mine, for all things.

30 Vino, primero, pura,
vestida de inocencia;
y la amé como un niño.
Luego se fué vistiendo
de no sé qué ropajes;
y la fuí odiando, sin saberlo.
Llegó a ser una reina,
fastuosa de tesoros . . .
¡Qué iracundia de yel y sin sentido!
. . . Mas se fué desnudando.
Y yo le sonreía.
Se quedó con la túnica
de su inocencia antigua.
Creí de nuevo en ella.
Y se quitó la túnica,
y apareció desnuda toda . . .
¡Oh pasión de mi vida, poesía
desnuda, mía para siempre!

Antolojía, 411.

31

AURORA

El amanecer tiene
esa tristeza de llegar,
en tren, a una estación que no es de uno.

¡Qué agrios los rumores
de un día que se sabe pasajero
—oh vida mía!—

—Arriba, con el alba, llora un niño.—

Antolojía, 420.

30 Maiden, at first she met me
all clothed in innocence,
and I loved her like a child.
Then she was dressing up
in goodness knows what fancies ;
I hated her, not knowing why.
She even became a queen,
magnificent in her treasures . . .
what gall and bitterness, and oh, what nonsense!
. . . Then she began undressing,
and I could smile upon her.
Soon she was left in her shift,
in her former innocence ;
I believed in her once more.
Then she took off even that
and appeared before me naked . . .
Oh, passion of all my life! Oh, poetry,
naked and mine forever!

31

AURORA

Daybreak brings along with it
that sad feeling of arrival
by train, at a railway station that isn't one's own.

How harshly sound the voices,
of a day one knows is merely transitory.
—oh, my dear life !

—Up there, now, with the daybreak a child's crying . . .

32

A DANTE

. . . Allegro sì, che appena il conoscìa . . .
Dante.

Tu soneto, lo mismo
que una mujer desnuda y casta,
sentándome en sus piernas puras,
me abrazó con sus brazos celestiales.

Soñé, después, con él, con ella.
Era una fuente
que dos chorros arqueaba en una taza
primera, la cual, luego, los vertía,
finos, en otros dos . . .

Antolojía, 434.

33

EL POEMA

Arranco de raíz la mata,
llena aún del rocío de la aurora.

¡Oh, qué riego de tierra
olorosa y mojada,
qué lluvia—¡qué ceguera!—de luceros
en mi frente, en mis ojos!

Antolojía, 466.

34

¡Qué inmensa desgarradura
la de mi vida en el todo,
para estar, con todo yo,
en cada cosa;
para no dejar de estar,
con todo yo, en cada cosa!

Antolojía, 469.

32 TO DANTE

Yours the sonnet, the likeness
of a fair woman chaste and naked
who took me on her knees and held me,
embracing me with celestial embraces.

And then I dreamed of it, and of her.
There was a fountain,
and two arching jets were spouting into a basin
above me, and then poured out their thin streams
into two other basins.

33 THE POEM

I plucked the whole plant, root and leaves,
dripping still with the dew of early morning.

Oh, how it watered the earth,
everywhere scented and moistened;
what raindrops, what a blinding fall of stars,
on my face, in my eyes!

34 How immense and ragged the rent,
torn in my life and in all things,
that I may be with all myself
in everything;
and that I never cease to be
with all myself in everything!

35 EL RECUERDO—4

¡Oh recuerdos secretos
fuera de los caminos
de todos los recuerdos!

¡Recuerdos, que una noche
de pronto, resurjís,
como una rosa en un desierto,
como una estrella al mediodía,
—pasión mayor del frío olvido—,
jalones de la vida
mejor de uno,
que casi no se vive!

¡Senda
diariamente árida;
maravilla, de pronto,
de primavera única,
de los recuerdos olvidados!

Antolojía, 471.

36 EL RECUERDO—5

El río pasa por debajo
de mi alma, socavándome.
Apenas me mantengo
en mí. No me sostiene
el cielo. Las estrellas
me engañan; no, no están
arriba, sino abajo, allá en el fondo . . .

¿Soy? ¡Seré!
Seré, hecho onda
del río del recuerdo . . .

¡Contigo, agua corriente!

Antolojía, 472.

35 MEMORY

Oh, memories in secret,
far off the winding pathways
of all my other memories!

The thought that in the night time
unlooked-for comes again,
strange as a wild rose in the desert,
strange as a star that shines at noonday,
—the agony of cold forgetting—
the rod and staff of all
that is most worth living,
the life scarce lived at all!

Always
the path is dull, arid;
then the miracle happens,
the only true springtime,
of all the memories once forgotten!

36 MEMORY

A stream is flowing in the depths
of my spirit, undermining me.
I can hardly maintain
my strength. No help comes to me
from heaven. Even stars
deceive me; none are there
above me, only below me, down in the depths.

Am I here? I *shall* be!
I shall—turned to a ripple
on the stream of memory.

Oh, running water, I'm with you!

37 A LA VEJEZ AMADA

¡Ay, si el recuerdo
tuyo de mí, fuese este cielo azul
de mayo, lleno todo
de las estrellas puras de mis actos!

¡De mis actos iguales, como ellas; todos puros,
limpios, buenos, tranquilos, igual que las estrellas!

—¡Debajo, tu sonrisa en sueños
—sueños de tus recuerdos de mi vida!—

Antolojía, 477.

38 CUESTA ARRIBA

¡Inmenso almendro en flor,
blanca la copa en el silencio pleno de la luna,
el tronco negro en la quietud total de la sombra;
cómo, subiendo por la roca agria a ti,
me parece que hundes tu troncón
en las entrañas de mi carne,
que estrellas con mi alma todo el cielo!

Antolojía, 482.

39 MARES

Siento que el barco mío
ha tropezado, allá en el fondo,
con algo grande.
¡Y nada
sucede! Nada . . . Quietud . . . Olas . . .

—¿Nada sucede; o es que ha sucedido todo,
y estamos ya, tranquilos, en lo nuevo?

Antolojía, 494.

37 AFTER MANY YEARS

If only the memory
you have of me were this blue vault of heaven
in May-time, hung all over
with the pure, shining stars of all my actions!

If my acts had been equal, as the stars are, all unsullied ;
limpid, good and tranquil, like the stars in their courses!

—And there I see you smiling in your dreams,
dreams that are all your memories of my life!—

38 HILL-TOP

The enormous almond in flower!
White to the top, in the great, full silence of white moonlight ;
the trunk all black in the total peace of the dark shadow.
So while I climbed up by the steep rock to you,
I thought that you plunged your great trunk
right to the depths of my being,
and starred the whole of heaven with my soul.

39 SEAS

I felt that my little boat
had run aground, and in the depths
lay some large object.
And nothing
had happened? Nothing . . . All still . . . Rollers . . .

Nothing had happened? Or was it that everything
had happened,
and we had come gently into a new world?

40 EPITAFIO IDEAL DE UN MARINERO

Hay que buscar, para saber
tu tumba, por el firmamento.
—Llueve tu muerte de una estrella.
La losa no te pesa, que es un universo
de ensueño—.
En la ignorancia, estás
en todo—cielo, mar y tierra—muerto.

Antolojía, 498.

41

El barco entra, opaco y negro,
en la negrura trasparente
del puerto inmenso.
Paz y frío.
—Los que esperan,
están aún dormidos con su sueño,
tibios en ellos, lejos todavía y yertos dentro de él,
de aquí, quizás . . .

¡Oh vela real nuestra, junto al sueño
de duda de los otros! ¡Seguridad, al lado
del sueño inquieto por nosotros!—

Paz. Silencio.
Silencio que, al romperse, con el alba,
hablará de otro modo.

Antolojía, 499.

40 EPITAPH ON AN UNKNOWN SAILOR

Look not on earth, you who would find
your grave, but in the firmament.
—It was a star rained death on you.
The stone shall not lie heavy ; it is a universe
of dream-stuff.—
In nescientness you dwell :
in all—in heaven, at sea, on earth—a dead man.

41 The boat came in, obscure and black,
through the transparent inky darkness
of the enormous harbour.
—Peace and cold.
Those who were waiting
were only half awake and full of slumber,
warm in them still, and far away, and rigid still within their
dream . . .
of presence there, perhaps ?

The watch we kept was real, beside the dream
of doubt which held the others. But they, at heart, were certain
in restless slumbers which we brought them.

Peace, Silence.
Silence that would be broken with the morning,
and would speak in another way.

42 Mariposa de luz,
la belleza se va cuando yo llego
a su rosa.

Corro, ciego, tras ella . . .
la medio cojo aquí y allá . . .

¡Sólo queda en mi mano
la forma de su huída!

Antolojía, 500.

43 ANTE LA SOMBRA VIRJEN

Siempre yo penetrándote,
pero tú siempre virjen,
sombra; como aquel día
en que primero vine
llamando a tu secreto,
cargado de afán libre.

¡Virjen oscura y plena
pasada de hondos iris
que apenas se ven; toda
negra, con las sublimes
estrellas, que no llegan
(arriba) a descubrirte!

Canción, 377.

42 Fritillary! Light!
But the beauty is gone when I arrive
at her rose.

Blindly, blindly pursue her . . .
Half catch her here, half catch her there . . .

All that's left in my hand :
the form of her flight!

43 BEFORE THE VIRGIN SHADOW

Perpetual penetration,
perpetual virginity—
shadow! Even as on that day
when first I came to see you
demanding of you your secret,
weighed down with boundless passion.

Virgin dark and mysterious,
stained to the iris depths
that are scarce to be seen ; all
black, with the sublimity
of stars that ever strive
up there, to find you here on earth.

44 AURORA DE TRASMUROS

A todo se le ve la cara, blanca
—cal, pesadilla, adobe, anemia, frío,—
contra el oriente. ¡Oh, cerca de la vida;
oh, duro de la vida! ¡Semejanza
animal en el cuerpo—raíz, escoria—,
—con el alma mal puesta todavía—,
y mineral y vegetal!
¡Sol yerto contra el hombre,
contra el cerdo, las coles y la tapia!
—¡Falsa alegría, porque estás tan sólo
en la hora—se dice—, no en el alma!

Todo el cielo tomado
por los montones humeantes, húmedos,
de los estercoleros horizontes.
Restos agrios, aquí y allá,
de la noche. Tajadas,
medio comidas, de la luna verde,
cristalitos de estrellas falsas,
papel mal arrancado, con su yeso aún fresco,
de cielo azul. Los pájaros,
aún mal despiertos, en la luna cruda,
farol casi apagado.
¡Recua de seres y de cosas!
—¡Tristeza verdadera, porque estás tan sólo
en el alma—se dice—no en la hora!—

Poesía, 87.

44 DAWN OUTSIDE THE WALLS

Everything bare and uncovered, all white—
plaster, nightmare, adobe, anaemia ; cold—
facing the east. How close it is to life ;
how hard the life is, too! An animal likeness
as touching the body—the root, the scoriae—
the soul still badly situated—
a likeness mineral and vegetable!
Sun striking down on men,
on pigs, on cabbage-stalks, on mud walls!
How false your gaiety, that are so lonely ;
lonely in time, perhaps, not in the soul.

The whole sky is enclosed
by vast and steaming mounds of damp manure,
the whole horizon ringed about with dung-heaps.
Rubbish scattered here and there :
last night's sweepings. Slices of food
only half eaten ; from a green mirror
crystal splinters of imitation stars ;
wall-paper roughly torn off, with the plaster clinging
(but sky-blue once!) The morning birds
still barely awake, in the crude white moonlight,
a street-lamp almost out.
Strange collection of things and people!
A sadness that is genuine, because so lonely ;
lonely in soul, you'd say, but not in time.

45 FIGURACIONES

¡Oh días de colores en la noche:
auroras—dalias de oro con rocío—
del túnel de los sueños;
cenites—techos májicos en llamas—
de la cueva del sueño;
—faisanes contra el ocaso grana—
ponientes de la cárcel del ensueño;
—. . . belleza involuntaria y tarda, siempre
para el desprevenido,
para el desconcertado; vida única!—

Belleza, 9.

45 FIGURATION

Oh, days that lend their colour to the night:
the daybreak—golden dahlias dripped with dew—
the tunnel's end of dream;
the zenith—magic ceiling wrapped in flames—
from the cavern of deep sleep;
—a golden pheasant in the crimson sunset—
a red sky from the prison-house of day-dreams:
—the beauty that's undesigned and tardy, always
there for the improvident,
there for the slovenly: the only kind of life!

46 LA PAZ

Cuando esta madrugada
abran las campanillas granas
a la luna dorada,
tú no estarás ya en casa,
sombra desnuda y blanca.

—Estarás noblemente
sosegada y risueña entre
la novedad alegre,
contenta de tu suerte
que te hace indiferente,
tras la vida, la muerte.—

Se irá encendiendo el día
con una luz tristísima ;
la brisa verde y fría
llenará, como un agua descendida,
la azotea vacía.

—. . . ¡Y habrá que levantarse,
y habrá que hacer ¡de prisa! las cosas matinales,
y habrá que ver y oír por todas partes
los gritos, las carreras, los alardes,
—¡sol en la pobre carne con su sangre!—,
las deslumbradas fealdades acres!

Belleza, 16.

46 PEACE

Before to-morrow's sunrise
every bell will be ringing red
to the gold of the moon ;
but you will not be at home then,
a white and naked shadow.

You will be housed more nobly,
rest and happiness round you,
in a new and bright existence
contented with your lot,
making you quite indifferent,
not in life but in death.

The day will grow light again,
but with light most melancholy ;
the wind blow green and cold,
overflow like the rain that pours in torrents
on the empty roof above.

And one will get up in the morning,
and have to do in a hurry the things of every morning,
and have to see and hear in every corner
the shouts, the running to and fro, the swanking—
—sun on the poor defenceless flesh and blood—
the dazzling light of bitter ugliness.

47 BALCÓN DE OTOÑO

En el alambre del teléfono
tiembla, verde neuróbata, una estrella.—
La ciudad, en el trueque del otoño,
es otra ciudad. Frescas
brisas dibujan los tejados,
—los postes del telégrafo, los pararrayos,
                    las cuerdas y las astas—,
sobre el ocaso de honda trasparencia.
—Una mujer y un gato, en la
baranda de una ¿jaula, puente de buque?,
                        no, azotea,
cortan sus breves
siluetas iguales y negras.—

¡Qué bien!—Las manos
en los bolsillos ya—. ¡Qué gusto! Eternas
variedades se ofrecen, repetidas,
al alma trasplantada a nueva escena.

La ciudad vira, flota, se desancla.
¿El mundo va por mar? ¿Dios es marino?

El momento me lleva,
¿en barco, en coche, en tren, en aeroplano?,
—todo corre, retiembla, jira, vuela—,
a mil puertos, a mil parques, a mil montañas
y mil ciudades nuevas.

Desde el balcón de par en par,
¡qué perspectivas ¡oh!
de eternidad alterna!

Belleza, 70.

47 BALCONY IN AUTUMN

Out on the long wire of the telephone
a large star quivers, a green dragon-fly.
The town, now autumn's here again,
becomes a new place. Breezes
pencil the outlines of the roofs
—the telegraph-poles, the lightning-conductors, the
lines and clothes-props—
seen in a sunset of deep transparency.
—Woman and cat lean out
from the gold bar of a bird-cage—the captain's bridge?
No, a roof-garden!
cutting off short
their equal and black-lined shadows.

That's right! Both hands
back in our pockets already. Delightful! How endless
are the varieties offered again and again
to the human soul transplanted to new pastures.

Now the town swings, is afloat, weighs anchor.
The whole world off to sea? God is a sailor?

Borne along by the moment
by ship or car or train or aeroplane,
all things running, vibrating, turning, flying—
to new harbours and new car-parks and new mountains
and new cities in thousands.

Out of the window open wide
what great perspective, ah!
vicarious eternity!

48 PACTO

El Guadarrama sale de la noche,
de azul mejor, de más gran rosa
bañado de desnudos infinitos,
con luz y norma
de incalculable eternidad.

No es nuestro todavía ni otra vez ;
aún, por sus aires hondos, está fuera
de nuestra relación ;
aún no ha llegado, en la usual escala,
a plantarse en el suelo ;
aún es de materiales de otro grado.

Cuando se una y se afiance
a la insubible superficie
de nuestra acostumbrada realidad
y sus caminos y sus aguas
encuentren su fusión rota en lo oscuro,
este húmedo teatro
de fachadas atónitas de aurora,
tapas de carne horizontal,
será Madrid de España ; y ese harapo
rojo, lacio, amarillo,
fin de una caja, cubos ahora huecos,
para hombres y mujeres,
será bandera y española . . . Al fin, nosotros,
coincidiremos con nosotros.

Y empezará otro día
vagamente obligado a su función,
en este inadecuado trasunto del vivir,
con la condescendencia maternal,
ajena, sonriente,
de la naturaleza insigne y grande.

La estación total.

48 PACTO

The Guadarrama comes out of the night
a bluer blue, a redder rose ;
stands there all bathed in bare infinities,
in light and pattern
of incalculable eternity.

Not yet is it ours, nor has it come again ;
but still in the deep-toned wind it lies apart
and out of touch with us ;
nor has it reached us on the normal scale,
to plant itself on the earth,
and still is formed of material of other nature.

Let it stand forth for surety
to that unclimbed and glittering surface
of our well-known familiar reality,
when all its ways and all its waters
have found their point of fusion gone in darkness ;
then this damp theatre
of house-fronts taken unaware by daylight,
coverings for horizontal flesh,
will be Madrid in Spain ; this tattered rag,
faded red and faded yellow,
on top of a box, a row of empty partitions,
—homes for men and for women—
this thing will be our national flag . . . For after all,
we can only be what we are.

So another day will begin,
vaguely conscious of duty to be done,
in this absurd, inadequate version of being alive ;
with a feeling of that maternal condescension,
so strange, yet so friendly,
of Nature that is something great and grand.

49 ROSA DE SOMBRA

Quien fuera no me vió, me vió su sombra
que vino justa, cálida a asomarse
por mi vida entreabierta,
esencia gris sin más olor ;
ola en donde dos ojos hechos uno se inmensaban.

Sombras que ven del todo, y no reciben
mirada. Nos alarman, mas son invulnerable-
mente tranquilas como aceite.

Con su espiralidad de escorzo exacto inventan
todo acto imposible de espionaje,
de introducción, de envolvimiento.

Sobrecojen sin miedo,
muerden sin labio,
se van sin compromiso.

A veces nos dejaron una rosa
esencia gris sin más olor,
prenda sensual de fe sin nombre.

Una rosa de sombras y de sombra,
alargada a mi mano esbeltamente,
con música sin son, con corrida sonrisa,
por cuerpo que no vió,
guardo en mi mano abierta.

La estación total.

49 ROSE OF THE SHADOW

Who saw me or saw me not, the shadow saw me.
It came just then, a man-warm shadow, creeping
through my life, the door half open,
an ash-grey essence, unperfumed,
a wave where two great eyes, made one, shone forth in
immensity.

Shadows : they see all round them, but never acknowledge
our glances. They alarm us ; but then, like oil,
remain invulnerably tranquil.

With their spirals winding in and out, and exact fore-
shortening,
predicting every impossible act of espionage,
of insinuation and intervention.

Apprehensive yet fearless,
biting yet lipless,
they leave no obligation.

At times, they leave a rose behind them,
an ash-grey essence unperfumed,
sensual pledge of a faith left nameless.

Sombre rose of the shadows, and formed from shadow,
set within reach of my hand with an elegant gesture,
with soundless melody, with shame-faced laughter,
by something that could not see—
here in my hand I hold it.

50

Quisiera que mi libro
fuese, como es el cielo por la noche,
todo verdad presente, sin historia.

Que, como él, se diera en cada instante,
todo, con todas sus estrellas ; sin
que niñez, juventud, vejez quitaran
ni pusieran encanto a su hermosura inmensa.

¡Temblor, relumbre, música
presentes y totales!
¡Temblor, relumbre, música en la frente
—cielo del corazón—del libro puro!

Antolojía, 522.

50 I would that all my verses
could be such as the sky is in the night-time :
truth of the moment—now—without history.

That, like the sky, they would yield at every instant
all things, with all their streaming stars, and
neither childhood, nor youth, nor age could rob them,
nor cast a spell on the immensity of their beauty.

A thrill, a bright flash, music,
before my eyes and upon me!
The thrill, the bright flash, the music, right between my eyes,
—the whole sky in my heart—the naked book!

EL TIGRE
(de William Blake)

(Querido J. B. Trend : no poseía todo Blake. Por su regalo del libro POETRY AND PROSE, terremoteador, que me ha conmovido continentes y mares, le mando esta traducción ideal del férreo segundo TYGER).

¡Tigre, tigre, que ardes vivo por los arbolados de la noche, ¿qué mano, qué ojo inmortal pudo organizar tu pavorosa simetría ?

¿En qué abismos, en qué firmamentos distantes llameaba el fuego de tus ojos ? ¿Con qué alas osó quién atreverse ? El fuego aquél, ¿qué mano se resolvió a cojerlo ?

¿Y qué hombro y qué maña pudo retorcer los tendones de tu corazón ? Y cuando tu corazón empezó a latir, ¿quién fué la terrible mano, quiénes los pies terribles ?

¿Cuál fué el martillo, cuál la cadena? ¿En qué fragua cayó tu cerebro? ¿Cuál fué el yunque? ¿Qué garra tremenda se arriesgó a apresar sus espantos mortales?

Cuando las estrellas arrojaron sus lanzas y regaron el cielo con sus lágrimas, ¿sonrió él mirando su obra ? ¿El que hizo al Cordero, te hizo a ti ?

¡Tigre, tigre, que ardes vivo por los arbolados de la noche, ¿ qué mano, qué ojo inmortal se decidió a cuajar tu pavorosa simetría ?

Juan Ramón Jiménez.
(*Madrid*, 1920)

Obra en marcha (*Diario poético*), *I* (1928).

Tyger! Tyger! burning bright
In the forests of the night,
What immortal hand or eye
Could frame thy fearful symmetry?

In what distant deeps or skies
Burnt the fire of thine eyes?
On what wings dare he aspire?
What the hand dare seize the fire?

And what shoulder, and what art,
Could twist the sinews of thy heart?
And when thy heart began to beat,
What dread hand? and what dread feet?

What the hammer? what the chain?
In what furnace was thy brain?
What the anvil? what dread grasp
Dare its deadly terrors clasp?

When the stars threw down their spears,
And water'd heaven with their tears,
Did he smile his work to see?
Did he who made the Lamb make thee?

Tyger! Tyger! burning bright
In the forests of the night,
What immortal hand or eye,
Dare frame thy fearful symmetry?

Blake.

INDEX OF FIRST LINES

www.ingramcontent.com/pod-product-compliance
Lightning Source LLC
Chambersburg PA
CBHW021705110726
47902CB00007B/2071

* 9 7 8 0 5 2 0 3 4 9 9 6 4 *